# A Heart Where Beauty Lives

### Alda Ellis

Harvest House Publishers
Eugene, Oregon

W9-CFI-791

## Dedication

To all the dedicated ladies and gentlemen
at Alda's Forever Soaps®—
for their beautiful hearts
filled with love and support
in my vision of building a successful
"people" business

## A Heart Where Beauty Lives

Copyright ©1999 by Alda Ellis
Published by Harvest House Publishers
Eugene, Oregon 97402

Library of Congress Cataloging-in-Publication Data

Ellis, Alda, 1952-
    A heart where beauty lives / Alda Ellis.
        p.    cm.
    ISBN 0-7369-0109-4
    1. Women—Conduct of life.  2. Ellis, Alda, 1952-    I. Title.
BJ1610.E55    1999                                    99-12832
248.8'43—dc21                                         CIP

Artwork which appears in this book is from
the personal collection of Alda Ellis.

Design and production by Left Coast Design, Portland, Oregon

Scripture quotations are from: the Holy Bible,
New International Version®. Copyright ©1973, 1978, 1984
by the International Bible Society. Used by permission of Zondervan
Publishing House; and the King James Version.

**Printed in China.**

99 00 01 02 03 04 05 06 07 08 / PP / 10 9 8 7 6 5 4 3 2 1

# Contents

# The Face of Beauty

*Be beautiful inside, in your hearts, with the lasting charm
of a gentle and quiet spirit which is so precious . . .*

THE BOOK OF 1 PETER

*I* was standing just inside
the door of my local department store, picking up
loose coins that had tumbled out when my
change purse fell open. To make matters worse, I
was trying to protect myself from the rain with a
contrary umbrella that had definite thoughts of its
own. Now that I was indoors, the umbrella naturally refused to close. Wondering if anyone would
assist me, I was surprised to see help arrive from
some unfamiliar faces. Several kind ladies actually
stooped down next to me to help me quickly
gather my coins. In the midst of the confusion, I
was a bit surprised that a frail, silver-haired lady
stopped, bent down to help, and offered words
of gentle humor while a young, bluejean-clad girl
only darted a brief glance at me as she quickly
passed by.

Now warm and dry inside the store, I strolled the aisles of the perfume department. I noticed the tremendously sophisticated marketing of products that were supposedly guaranteed to drastically improve every woman's appearance. Instantaneously absorbed in the promotions, posters, and campaigns of tote bags brimming with pretty tissue papers and attractive products, I almost forgot what I had come to buy. "Beauty's in a bottle and youth's in a jar" the captivating displays seemed to announce, but after my encounter with the elderly lady who helped me pick up my coins, I believe I had seen the true face of beauty.

Maybe you also have had the experience of seeing someone who you thought was quite beautiful from a distance or on the surface. Then you saw that same person react to a

*The best part of beauty is that which no picture can express...*

BACON

situation in a way that completely changed your initial impression of her, as well as your previous admiration of her beauty. Disagreeable tempers and unfriendly faces have no beauty about them. But a kind smile and an encouraging glance instantly transform an ordinary face into one of exquisite comeliness.

When I was in the third grade, I thought that my teacher was extraordinarily pretty. She was the kindest, most patient woman who once discreetly gave the red-headed, freckle-faced boy who sat in the seat behind me a brand-new pair of jeans. She knew that he had been wearing the same pair for weeks. It was a loving gesture to a young boy whose father had left the family and whose hard-working mother struggled to simply put food on the table. Our teacher knew how innocently uncaring we third graders could be with our simplistic honesty, and so she remedied the potential problem in her own quiet and unassuming way.

Only years later, as I flipped through the timeworn pages of my grade school photo album, did I see how plain my teacher really looked. In the picture I have of our class, I notice first that she had a gentle smile. Her hair was pulled neatly back and a painter's collar blouse framed her face. Although she appeared simple, her heart was anything but. She had taught us not only arithmetic, spelling, and handwriting, but also kindness, compassion, wisdom, and grace. Through my adoring third grade eyes, I had seen her as she really was—beautiful, simply beautiful—for I saw her with my heart.

*A thing of beauty is a joy forever; Its loveliness increases; it can never pass into nothingness.*

KEATS

True inward and outward beauty should be almost impossible to distinguish between, as one echoes the other. Cheeks glowing with a blush of peaches may only whisper of a woman's tender inner spirit. Never mind a milky, porcelain complexion, shiny chestnut tresses, or a smile that could stir music in the soul, for it is only with the heart that we can see what is invisible to the eye. True beauty is not merely skin deep; it originates clear down in the depths of the soul.

One of the hardest things to do is to look beyond our own mirror and assess the true attributes of beauty as, through the ages, they have stood the test of time. The most beautiful of faces may now be adorned with wrinkles, but the eyes radiate a warmth and a smile that breaks forth like the morning light. Some good advice to heed is to live your life without concentrating on your age. You *can* become more beautiful as you grow older.

The most beautiful of all women seem to have in common some timeless qualities of beauty—grace, wisdom, thoughtfulness, kindness, compassion— and they carry them with a certain sense of confidence. These are the qualities of what I believe to be true beauty. They are accessible to every woman. We need only to put them on and live our lives sheathed in their presence.

*Never lose an opportunity of seeing anything that is beautiful, for beauty is God's handwriting—a wayside sacrament. Welcome it in every fair face, in every fair sky, in every flower, and thank God for it as a cup of blessing.*

RALPH WALDO EMERSON

Grace

Gracefulness has been defined to be the outward expression of the inward harmony of the soul.

WILLIAM HAZLITT

*G*race has been defined as unmerited help, or the ease of movement adding beauty and charm to the mundane tasks of the day. Grace is also a prayer that is said before mealtime. Having grace means showing dignity and elegance, attributes that are demonstrated through what we call "manners." Grace is such an admirable quality that it is the subject of one of our best-loved hymns, "Amazing Grace." Within the words of the song we are reminded of the most important meaning of grace—the act of proffering a loving heart to someone who might not deserve it or, more importantly, likely has not earned it.

*Gifts are what a man has, but Graces are what a man is.*

F.W. ROBERTSON

When I think of grace, I think of a woman who lived her life by it. Queen Victoria of England left behind a legacy as one of the most graceful monarchs to have ever ruled a kingdom. Throughout her reign, Victoria held fast to a deep reverence for her God, her family, and her country. She brought with her to the throne a sacredness to the tasks of raising a family and ruling a people. Affectionate as an adoring wife and dutiful mother, she became a worldwide example of grace and goodness. And so it was through her day-to-day rituals that she set forth in ruling not only a country, but her children as well. She forgave her subjects as

she lovingly
forgave her children,
showing them mercy,
compassion, and grace.

Within grace lies the spirit of
forgiveness. To me, this can be
one of the most difficult challenges
to developing true beauty. Try as I might,
I sometimes cannot cast from my memory the
times when I was wronged
by someone I loved and
trusted. Recently, through
my day-to-day experiences
of owning and operating a
business, someone I had
placed much faith in dis-
appointed me and let me
down. Although it hurt me
deeply, I realize that at
times I, too, have let others down, perhaps without
my even knowing it.
Sometimes it is most
difficult to ask those we
have wronged to forgive us. But when we do, it
reflects the beauty of our character and heart. And
it is through prayer and the grace of God that we
can forgive those who have hurt us.

*Her angel's face*
*As the great eye of heaven*
*  shined bright,*
*And made a sunshine in*
*  the shady place;*
*Did never mortal eye*
*  behold such heavenly*
*  grace.*

EDMUND SPENSER

Clara Barton, founder of the American Red Cross, was a woman of uncommon courage, insight, and grace. Many stories have been recorded about her fascinating life. One story I love to recall is one in which a friend reminds Clara of a vicious deed that a coworker had rendered her years before. "Don't you remember what she did to you, Clara?" the friend asks, recalling the painful situation.

"No," Clara replies, "I don't. But I do distinctly remember forgetting it."

Grace is perhaps the most important of all attributes, for without forgiveness we carry bitterness in our hearts, which is most destructive. Yet grace replaces the bitterness with healing love.

A smile may only take a moment to impart, but the memory of it can last forever. Likewise, a word of forgiveness or a heartfelt apology costs nothing, yet its rewards are great. For those who receive it are the richer without making poorer of those who give. Forgiveness is everything. Grace is beauty.

*Holy, fair, and*
*wise is she;*
*The heaven such grace*
*did lend her,*
*That she might*
*admired be.*

WILLIAM
SHAKESPEARE

Wisdom

> For Wisdom
> is more precious
> than rubies, and
> nothing you desire
> can compare with her.
>
> THE BOOK OF
> PROVERBS

*F*rom time to time I have pondered the question, "Would you rather have wisdom, or would you rather have youth?" The question implies that the two cannot dwell in a person at the same time, and that certainly gives us something to think about. My mother once said that the difference between education and wisdom was that education was learned and wisdom was earned. Many people have been blessed with an abundance of education but still have not earned wisdom, for wisdom has

> *Wisdom is oft times nearer when we stoop than when we soar.*
>
> WILLIAM WORDSWORTH

a price that costs more than money can buy—it costs us our youth. The secret therein lies that by gaining wisdom, we can indeed become more beautiful with age.

*Strength and honor are her clothing; and she shall rejoice in time to come. She openeth her mouth with wisdom: and in her tongue is the law of kindness.*

THE BOOK
OF PROVERBS

Along with wisdom come the qualities of understanding and patience—knowing when to speak, and knowing when to be silent. It is said that it is better to be quiet and be thought a fool than to speak and remove all doubt. In other words, if I think ahead of time about what I am going to say and how I am going to react, I most likely will not have to apologize for the wrong words coming out of my mouth.

I learned a valuable lesson about wisdom early on in my professional life. I had just graduated from college with my degree in dental hygiene and landed what I imagined as the perfect job for me. I was working in an office near my home and friends. The hours were wonderful, the people were friendly, and I quickly became good friends with everyone on the staff.

One afternoon I returned to the office a little early from lunch. I was trying to lend a hand by doing some extra cleaning of the cabinet tops in the lab. In the midst of my chore, a mold with a porcelain tooth slipped from my hand and shattered on the floor. Since I was so new to the office, I was uncertain of how the dentist for whom I worked would react to my error. I opened his office door with the porcelain fragments in my cupped hands and my head bowed. I explained that in the process of cleaning I had

*Be careful, then how you live—not as unwise but as wise, making the most of every opportunity.*

THE BOOK
OF EPHESIANS

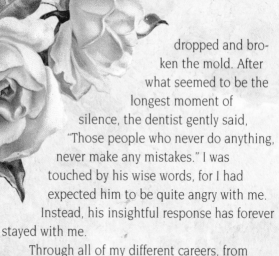

dropped and broken the mold. After what seemed to be the longest moment of silence, the dentist gently said, "Those people who never do anything, never make any mistakes." I was touched by his wise words, for I had expected him to be quite angry with me. Instead, his insightful response has forever stayed with me.

Through all of my different careers, from working at the dental office to being a stay-at-home mom to running a business, I have never forgotten the dentist's words. More than once they have held my temper in check, reminding me to be slow to anger when frustrated with a friend or family member. Perhaps my sons have seen the wisdom of withholding one's anger when they were trying to help me and broke a treasured trinket. For I have always tried to react with wisdom.

Honesty and strength both exist within the realm of wisdom, for we all face times when we must stand for what is right

*Be wise in using the tools God gives you, for just as the hammer builds a house, it shatters glass.*

ALDA ELLIS

with courage. Through the years this prayer has been offered over and over in difficult situations that require an abundance of wisdom: "God grant me the Serenity to accept the things I cannot change, the Courage to change the things I can, and the Wisdom to know the difference. Amen."

To find wisdom is to embark upon a quest for truth and honesty. And no matter what our age, we must continue our quest. It has taken me a lifetime to understand the wisdom of what is called the "good life." As I carry on with my personal quest for beauty, pearls of wisdom are offered to me by others. Sometimes they are presented as things that I must ponder. Sometimes they are simply placed upon my heart when I have taken the time to listen. Even though I have a college degree, a nice home, a nice car, and a job I love, I know that these things do not bring me wisdom. For without the knowledge that God loves me, my husband loves me, and my children love me, the material things of the good life, even though they are wonderful, would never fill my heart as satisfyingly as the warmth of those who surround me. By knowing this, I understand that there is beauty in wisdom.

*Thoughtfulness*

*T*houghtfulness is one
of beauty's most caring aspects, for when we are
thoughtful we say that we care. Actions speak so
much louder than words, and so it is with my
friend Dot. She is one of the most beautiful ladies
I know, and thoughtfulness is certainly her trade-
mark virtue.

Dot lives far away from me, but I know I am
in her thoughts by the considerate things she
does. Unexpected cards from Dot often arrive in
my mail. She works as a nurse and has a very
busy schedule with family and grandchildren as
well, but she always takes the time to jot down
a word of encouragement on a pretty card and
surprise me with it. Her little gifts of love bring a
smile to my face and a warmth to my heart as I
realize that she was thinking of me during her
busy day.

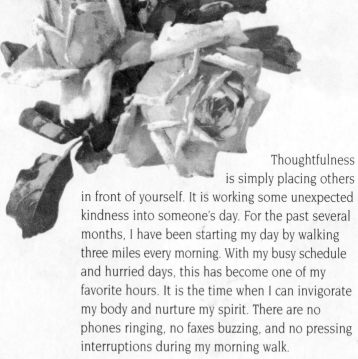

Thoughtfulness is simply placing others in front of yourself. It is working some unexpected kindness into someone's day. For the past several months, I have been starting my day by walking three miles every morning. With my busy schedule and hurried days, this has become one of my favorite hours. It is the time when I can invigorate my body and nurture my spirit. There are no phones ringing, no faxes buzzing, and no pressing interruptions during my morning walk.

I call this hour my gift of the day, for it is during this time that I organize my thoughts and say my prayers. And it is during this time that I plan at least one act of thoughtfulness for someone else. My acts are often quite small, perhaps just calling to check in on someone or sending a card or running an errand. But I try to let those around me know that they are loved, and I show this love not only by my words but

*Deeds, not words, shall speak me.*

JOHN FLETCHER

also by my actions. In fact, I believe that I can tell someone I love them without ever saying a word.

Sometimes thoughtfulness is a show of beauty in the truest sense of the word. Fifteen years ago the area in which we live was hit by a tornado. Thank goodness I was not in the house when the storm blew over, for I think it would have frightened me beyond belief. Huge hundred-year-old oak trees were lying on the ground as if they were spilled toothpicks. The devastation was humbling.

*A merry heart doeth good like medicine.*

THE BOOK OF PROVERBS

As I made my way through telephone poles scattered in the streets and drove my car as close to my house as I could, I remember feeling as numb as the rainy, cold skies. Approaching the house, I saw my husband standing in our driveway looking at the trees lying around and on our home. I threw my arms around him, so thankful that we were

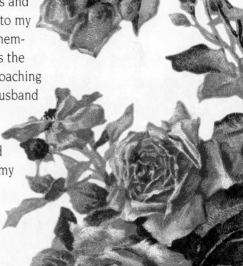

both safe. Then I noticed the hum of a chainsaw. To our amazement the man behind the chainsaw was David, a friend we hadn't seen in years. He was on his way home from work and stopped when he saw what the trees had done to our home. Even though David did not see us, he was nonetheless out in the rain cutting up the trees to help us put things back together. I will always treasure in my heart his thoughtful act and generous gift of time when we least expected it.

*Words are also actions, and actions are a kind of words.*

RALPH WALDO EMERSON

An interesting reward to being thoughtful is that it has actual benefits to our health. Studies have shown that helping others most likely reduces stress and promotes good health. It seems that selfless activities such as volunteering or tutoring produce a sense of well-being in the body. So it seems that being thoughtful produces not only a beautiful spirit, but aids in physical health, too. And the rewards of thoughtfulness are everlasting.

*Kindness*

*I*f there is anything this
world needs more of, it is kindness. Kindness has
its quiet yet enduring allure of beauty, a kind of
beauty that is unseen and is only felt with the
heart. Kindness is that brief moment when something precious touches our soul and stays with us
when we walk away. It is given freely for no partic-
ular reason and with nothing expected in return.

Kindness is an attitude that plays out in how
we carry on with our daily deeds. When we are
raising our children, caring for our spouses, and
working hard at our jobs day by day, it is the spirit
in which we carry out the ordinary that speaks of
kindness.

One day my son Samuel forgot his lunch
box as he hurried out the door in the rush of yet
another school morning. The school secretary
phoned later that morning and I told her I would
drop his lunch by the office. At first I was irritated

*Guard within yourself that treasure, Kindness. Know how to give without hesitation, how to lose without regret, how to acquire without meanness: know how to replace in your heart, by the happiness of those you love, the happiness that may be wanting to yourself.*

GEORGE SAND

that he had forgotten it, as I had a very busy morning scheduled. But I let my anger melt away as I enclosed a note with the lunch that said, "Hope you have a great day. Love, Mother." For this was just another opportunity to tell my child that I loved him. And so it is with acts of kindness. The one who gives is actually twice blessed. The world around you is a little better for the kindness, and the giver's heart is blessed within.

For almost two weeks I had tried to shoo away a stray dog that refused to leave its newly claimed spot beside our barn. My own two dogs didn't even bark at the uninvited guest any-more, accepting that she was always there. Looking closer, I could see that the chow-mix breed had been badly mistreated and was simply too weak to

*If there is any kindness I can show, or any good thing I can do to any fellow being, let me do it now, and not deter or neglect it, as I shall not pass this way again.*

WILLIAM PENN

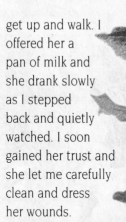

get up and walk. I offered her a pan of milk and she drank slowly as I stepped back and quietly watched. I soon gained her trust and she let me carefully clean and dress her wounds.

We gave her a name, Chow-Chow, and she eventually regained her dignity as she healed not only her wounds but also her heart. That happened two years ago, and Chow-Chow is now my constant companion. I sit on the patio and she always places her head in my lap, requesting that her ears be rubbed. Living with us in the country, she has mended her broken trust. As if to return the favor of days gone by, she is always by my side as I walk through the woods. A simple act of kindness rewarded me with the priceless gift of a lifelong friend.

Kindness cannot be taught from a book. It must be lived by example. Even the Girl Scout oath I took as a child modeled kindness: "Be kind in thought and word and deed." It was aptly demonstrated by our leaders as they showed us the importance of volunteer community service and taught us to learn by doing instead of merely repeating.

One Sunday I was involved in a disagreement with my oldest son, who was very busy with school activities, music lessons, and youth group meetings. He asked if he could spend his afternoon collecting cans for a school food drive, and I wanted him to stay home with the family. He was willing to give of his time, yet I wanted to enjoy his company at home for a savored Sunday afternoon. After I granted him permission to go collect the cans, I was glad I had done so. I had a son who

*What do we live for, if not to make the world less difficult for each other?*

GEORGE ELIOT

was willing to invest in others. The giving of his time was of little expense. It cost nothing, yet it brought such rich, rewarding dividends of the heart to the investor.

As our days unfold and in whatever they bring, we will be the one most blessed by including acts of kindness in our daily rituals. Whether caring for a family, a community, or a stray animal, the rewards of a kind heart reflect the soul's beauty.

*Life is short and we have not too much time for gladdening the hearts of those who are traveling the dark way with us. Oh, be swift to love! Make haste to be kind.*

HENRI FREDERIC
AMIEL

*Compassion*

*The dew of
compassion
is a tear.*

LORD
BYRON

*C*ompassion is an attribute of a woman's inner beauty, for it lies deep within one's being to the beating of the heart. I must tell you that once you truly have compassion, you will never again be quite the same. Compassion requires a sharing which carries with it tremendous responsibilities. The more of it you have, the greater becomes your capacity to give unto others.

My oldest son was assigned to write a school report on Mother Teresa of Calcutta. Perhaps her life itself was a study in compassion. If you look at a photograph of her, you can gaze into her eyes and read between the wrinkles the beautiful

*I*t is more blessed to give than to receive.

THE BOOK
OF ACTS

spirit of compassion that she embodied. The words on a page can ne'er do justice to the life of love and compassion she lived.

My business travels have taken me to her corner of the world, to the land and to the people whom she so desperately loved. And the journey I took to her beloved country forever changed me. I saw firsthand what she encountered on a daily basis—the day-to-day struggle for food, for clean water, for life. My two sons accompanied me on that trip, and they too came back with changed hearts.

The compassion which overcame us illustrated that heartache has no boundaries, no language barrier, no skin color, no country of origin. The more we saw of Mother Teresa's world, the more it made our hearts alive with thankfulness for how God had blessed us in our daily lives—a warm home, food abundant, and pure, clean water.

*Do all the good you can,*
*By all the means you can,*
*In all the ways you can,*
*In all the places you can,*
*At all the times you can,*
*To all the people you can,*
*As long as you ever can.*

JOHN WESLEY

The compassion I felt made me a more responsible wife, mother, and business owner. My life in business has given me many new discoveries of living and growing, but none quite like my experience abroad. The compassion I felt in that distinct moment of awareness has filtered into every step of my days. It has made me thankful for the things that I so often took for granted. And as I returned to my world, so blessed, I came home forever changed.

Every day on my

way to the office, I pass a panhandler on the street corner. I always used to glance away, reasoning to myself, "Well, he could work some-where and earn a living if he really wanted to." The traffic light would change to green and off I would go, dismissing the thought of him. But compassion cannot forget.

My mother lived life with a different attitude. I used to get so frustrated with her, for even though she was on a fixed income, she was forever sending five dollars to this mission project or ten dollars to that plea for funds. Her mail was filled with financial requests from all sorts of causes. Now Mother is gone, but the example of compassion she lived remains with me today. She reminded me that God had given her the responsi-bility to give, and that some-day she would have to answer for all of her actions. It was the responsibility of those to whom she gave to be honest in their receiving for

*Put on a heart of compassion*

THE BOOK
OF COLOSSIANS

they, too, would have to answer for their actions. No matter how much or how little we had, Mother believed we were always to be compassionate and giving. Compassion, great or small, was an act of giving herself to others. Returning from my lesson abroad and remembering the gentle teaching of my mother, I now see the street corner man through different eyes. Somehow he serves as my reminder. I must be responsible for my actions, and the beggar man must be accountable for his. Our paths cross once more, and I press a bill into his cup, but what I have really given is compassion.

Confidence

*C*onfidence is a warm cloak that adorns the shoulders of those who welcome into their lives the attributes of grace, wisdom, thoughtfulness, kindness, and compassion. Confidence allows the bearer to walk in beauty. It brings full circle the heart where beauty lives.

Well-placed confidence is rooted in faith, and so it is with whatever obstacles come my way. I can face the road I walk, for my walk is not alone. I do not always know where my path will lead, but with faith in my heart and confidence resting upon my shoulders, I know with whom I am going. In the movie *The Wizard of Oz,* the character of Dorothy

*The block of granite which is an obstacle in the pathway of the weak, becomes a stepping-stone in the pathway of the strong.*

THOMAS CARLYLE

clutches her heart at the end of her ordeal and exclaims, "Oh, Auntie Em! Oh, Auntie Em! I had the answer here in my heart all along." But as we all know, Dorothy set out without faith and her journey home made for a most interesting story.

*I can do all things through Christ who strengthens me.* I keep this verse from the Book of Philippians written on the first page of my journal. Even though the verse is short and I have etched it upon my heart to recite easily, at times it greatly helps me to see the words written down on paper. They serve as a gentle reminder of my faith and the well from which I draw confidence.

*It is not so much our friend's help that helps us as the confidence of their help.*

EPICURUS

We must be careful with confidence to not let pride enter, lest we lose the other attributes of beauty. I was once asked why I was so successful in turning a business that began with me making soap on my kitchen stove into a thriving wholesale company. My answer was that I did not have all the answers. My educational degree was not in business or marketing. I had no special training or skills. I experienced all of the disappointments, problems, and difficulties that go hand-in-hand with starting a business. Yet I had my little slip of paper as a reminder of faith and confidence.

And even though the company I began is now up and running, it doesn't mean that life is any easier. It just means that the problems are larger and the difficulties more abundant and the mistakes more

costly. If anyone told me ten years ago what I would be doing today, I am sure my reply would have been, "There is no way!"

Once when I was quite young, before I could even read, a Sunday school teacher told our class to hold out our hands. She said she was going to give each of us something that could get us anything in the world. As we sat in tiny green chairs neatly arranged in a circle, we each held out cupped little hands. The teacher placed something in them, then gently folded our fingers back up so that we would grasp it tightly. The object was so small that I remember thinking, "I don't think she put anything in my hand." Yet I kept my hands closed firmly along with all the other children. After everyone had gotten their special something, she said, "All right, now you may open your hands."

We unfurled our fingers to find something so tiny it seemed a mere speck. The speck in our hands, the teacher informed us, was a mustard seed. She shared with us that if we had faith even as tiny as that mustard seed, we could accomplish anything in the world we wanted to accomplish.

To us children, we imagined eating all the ice

*If ye have faith as a grain of mustard seed, nothing shall be impossible unto you.*

THE BOOK
OF MATTHEW

cream we wanted or staying up hours past our bedtime. And as our childish desires grew and matured, the message of the mustard seed stayed the same, for the secret was timeless and ageless. My ten-year journey of starting and growing a business was taken one single step at a time, my hands still clutching the reminder of the seed of faith.

It is said that the journey of a thousand miles begins with the first step. So too does my journey of the coming years begin with my reminder of mustard seed faith amid the passage of time. Clothed in a cloak of confidence, I will carry my slip of crumpled, timeworn paper with my life promise along with my tiny seed. And I will meet each new day with the beauty of confidence.

*Look for the beauty of others, and they will find the beauty in you.*

ALDA ELLIS

# *Pearls*

*Beauty is not caused. It is.*

EMILY DICKINSON

*I* love to see a woman wearing pearls, no matter if they are treasured family heirlooms or the dimestore variety. Ralph Waldo Emerson called them "the only gem that pales the moon." Grace, wisdom, thoughtfulness, kindness, compassion, and confidence have been called "pearls of wisdom," as they highlight the attributes of inner beauty. To me, pearls symbolize the true state of a woman's heart. Perhaps this is because they are just naturally beautiful. They need no polishing, no cutting; they are simply beautiful as they are.

> *True beauty is on the inside...Remember, the pearl always grows on the inside of the shell.*
>
> ALDA ELLIS

And so it is with the beauty within. The heart's beauty is timeless. It can do what no lipstick, powder, miracle cream, or even facelift can do. It creates a glowing fire from within that radiates the smile on a woman's face, illuminates the sparkle in her eyes, and warms the glow in her cheeks.

May we be reminded each time we slip a strand of pearls around our neck and fasten the fragile clasp that the most valued pearls are not the ones that cost the most. Rather, they are the pearls that reflect the most timeless qualities of beauty—grace, wisdom, thoughtfulness, kindness, compassion, and confidence. These pearls not only beautify our hearts but also make the world around us a more attractive place.

*There is no beautifier of complexion, or form or behavior, like the wish to scatter joy and not pain around us.*

RALPH WALDO
EMERSON

Some pearls are just artificial glass beads, designed to look like the real thing. The most beautiful ornaments of all, though, are the pearls in which troubles, toils, and snares have turned a grain of sand into a true and treasured gem. When darkness falls, *this* is the pearl that pales the moonlight.